PROTECT AND SERVE

By Santos Vallejo

Mr. Landward was a man that did everything right,
a handsome young man who lived with his wife.
He woke up each morning with a song on his lips,
a skip in his step and his K9 dog by his hip.

He loved his clothes neatly pressed for duty.
His wife would say, "You look good in that suit, Mr. Cutie."

For breakfast, Mr. Lanward worked on the cereal box puzzle. Even his K9 would help by fetching his pen.

"Hop in, Hop in." Mr. Lanward would say to his K9,
and together, they would ride off.
Each day was different yet full of adventure!

The wind would blow in K9's face,
full of excitement, he rode with his tongue out sideways.

Suddenly, a car brakes fast in front of Mr. Lanward
"Why do people do that?" He questioned in frustration.
"That's how accidents happen."

Paying for parking did not bother Mr. Lanward.

He confidently walks into the coffee shop waving a big hello.
Yet, no one said hi. They felt fear and hung their heads low.

This didn't bother Mr. Lanward one bit.
He would stay and at the end even leave a big tip.

With a big caring heart,
he held open the coffee shop door. " Come in, come in!"
Mr. Lanward kindly gestured to a mother with her child.

Then he heard something rather disturbing.
The mother was yelling at her daughter, " If you don't behave, that man in the suit will take you away!"

Staring at his suit the little girl was in fear.
Mr. Lanward saw her cheeks covered in tears,
and felt sadness in his heart.

Nevertheless, Mr. Lanward and K9 continued their duty. All of a sudden, they got an urgent call of a missing little girl.

It was getting dark, so they were in a hurry.
hey stopped at a nearby park where the little girl was last seen.
With the help of his K9,
they searched for a little girl
wearing a pink dress.

They searched everywhere imaginable,
yet they couldn't find her.
Mr. Lanward heard a whimper nearby yet wouldn't come out.
" I'm here to help!"
Mr.Lanward yelled out. The little girl saw Mr. Lanwards suit an
remembered him from the coffee shop. So, she hid even further.

Mr. Lanward found a pink bow and realizes he could be close. She still might not come out due to fear.

After his K9 sniffs the bow, he jumps into action and found the little girl. She still seemed to be a little scared.

Mr. Landward reunites the little girl with her mother.
He smiles when he sees them together.

The mother asked Mr. Lanward for forgiveness because of the remarks she made at the coffee shop.

"It's ok, I'm here to protect and serve."

The End